Original title:
The Quiet of Paradise

Copyright © 2025 Creative Arts Management OÜ
All rights reserved.

Author: Olivia Sterling
ISBN HARDBACK: 978-1-80581-628-7
ISBN PAPERBACK: 978-1-80581-155-8
ISBN EBOOK: 978-1-80581-628-7

A Sojourn in Restful Light

In a land where whispers sway,
Sunbeams dance and kids play.
The grass tickles our toes,
While a squirrel steals our clothes.

Ice cream melts in a sunny cone,
A dog steals fries but leaves the bone.
Laughter echoes through the trees,
Even the honeybees giggle in the breeze.

Chasing clouds that look like sheep,
We nap on pillows soft and deep.
A turtle jogs by, oh so slow,
Says, 'You kids, just take it slow!'

As evening wraps us in a hug,
We share our tales, each blissful slug.
The stars above wink with delight,
In this jaunt, everything feels just right.

Beyond the Clouds of Noise

In a world where silence reigns,
We dance where joy spills like rains.
A cat wears shades like a rockstar,
While a pig dreams of being a car.

The trees gossip with a flair,
As a frog jumps, we stop and stare.
Butterflies flutter, dressed to impress,
Even the mushrooms party, no less!

A raccoon in a tux, what a sight,
Holding a feast under the moonlight.
Every breeze brings laughter anew,
As the night sky turns a goofy hue.

With jokes that fly like silly kites,
We twirl and spin, embracing delights.
In this land of calm and cheer,
Everything's funny when friends are near.

Beneath the Canopy of Serenity

Beneath the trees, where squirrels dance,
The birds debate, should they take a chance.
A rabbit hops in a fancy hat,
While butterflies giggle, "What about that?"

A breeze whispers jokes to the flowers bright,
The daisies chuckle, 'This feels just right!'
A frog in a tie croaks a comedic tune,
As shadows play hide-and-seek with the moon.

The Solitude of Enchanted Groves

In the forest, where shadows tickle the ground,
A fox in sneakers makes the silliest sound.
Trees wear their leaves like oversized hats,
While crickets put on shows, performing acrobats.

A turtle in shades thinks he's the cool guy,
As butterflies laugh, soaring up high.
Raccoons threw a party, snacks piled so high,
But the owl just yawns, "Oh, please don't even try."

Embracing the Breath of Nature

In the meadow, a goat with a mischievous grin,
Strategizes ways to sneak in and win.
Grasshoppers cheer as it leaps with flair,
While bees hum a tune, dancing through the air.

A frog rehearses, "I can sing, I swear!"
Then croaks out a note that creates quite a scare.
But the daisies just sway, enjoying the tease,
As nature's quirks bring the heart to ease.

The Dew-Kissed Stillness

Morning breaks with a sparkle so bright,
A snail's on a journey, but moves at a fright.
"Hey, slow down buddy!" calls a butterfly in style,
While the dew drops giggle, "We'll wait for a while."

A kitten appears, pouncing here and there,
Chasing her shadow, without a single care.
The sun beams awake, showering warmth with glee,
As nature's own comedy unfolds carefree.

Within the Whispering Woods

In the woods where squirrels conspire,
Trees gossip low, they never tire.
A rabbit wears a tiny hat,
While deer dance like they're on a mat.

The mushrooms giggle, a colorful crew,
Telling secrets just to you.
A bear attempts to do the twist,
But trips and falls, oh, what a list!

A Pause for Reflection

In the pond where frogs compete,
A turtle's encore can't be beat.
He strikes a pose with a tiny smile,
While fish flip-flop; what a style!

A dragonfly zooms with flair,
Chasing his dreams through the air.
All this drama, oh what fun,
Time for a snack, hey, everyone!

Traces of Harmony

In the garden, the daisies prance,
Sunflowers join in a silly dance.
The wind teases, pulls at their rays,
As bumblebees buzz in a daze.

A ladybug lost, can't find her home,
Thinks she'll sit on a garden gnome.
But the gnome just sneezes, oh dear me,
Leaving our bug in a state of glee!

Secrets in the Silence

Beneath the branches, whispers soar,
A hedgehog giggles, rolls on the floor.
He tells a tale that no one believes,
Of a fox who wears bootlegged sleeves.

A snail writes tales, oh so grand,
Of adventures across the land.
But he'll take ages to reach the end,
Much like a tortoise, a slow friend!

Between the Leaves

Whispers tickle through the trees,
A squirrel's dance brings me to tease.
In every rustle, laughter hides,
As nature plots its joyful rides.

The grass giggles, sways with glee,
While flowers play a symphony.
A butterfly in silly flight,
Mocks the birds' off-key delight.

Silence Grows

In the hush, a frog does croak,
It leaps and lands; my sides are poked.
A snail races with a distant sigh,
While ants parade in line, oh my!

The calm stretches, legs unwind,
A bumblebee buzzes, never blind.
It bumps a petal, does a spin,
As laughter bubbles from within.

Surrender to Stillness

A lizard lounges, sunbathing wide,
While bees strike poses, full of pride.
A caterpillar takes a nap,
Dreaming of its future flap.

The clouds compose a cotton joke,
As shadows play while sunbeams poke.
In this calm, absurdities thrive,
Each moment makes my heart contrive.

An Oasis of Softness

Feathers fall from a high tree loft,
A pigeon glares, its judgment soft.
The wind tickles a sleepy pup,
As he dreams of a mishap sup.

A sandy beach sparks giggles low,
As crabs in tuxedos steal the show.
With each wave, they slip and slide,
A comedy of crusted pride.

Tides of the Unheard

In the distance, a turtle trumps,
Echoes of laughter, tiny jerks and jumps.
As waves chuckle at their own embrace,
Whispers weave a silly lace.

The horizon sways with a wink,
Seashells conspire, what do you think?
They plot to hide a piece of sand,
While a gull swoops down, bold and grand.

Elysian Dreams

In fields where giggles grow so tall,
A sheep in sunglasses starts to sprawl.
With daisies dancing, oh what a scene,
A chicken's cluck sounds so serene.

Butterflies flutter with fancy wings,
While frogs conspire to make funny things.
A snail in a race, losing with flair,
Who knew such laughter was floating in air?

Landscapes of Lull

A fern in a hat thinks it's quite grand,
While earthworms cheer with a marching band.
Clouds form shapes that tickle the mind,
A toaster in a tree—how rare to find!

The river giggles, splashing away,
Fish cracking jokes, oh what a play.
As sunbeams tickle each little leaf,
The joy around is beyond belief.

Closing Eyes in Nature's Lap

Close your eyes, hear a pebble's joke,
As crickets laugh and the owls provoke.
A squirrel jumps by with a nut on his head,
While ants plan a feast; I think I'm misled.

Dreams swirl like leaves in a light summer breeze,
And worms throw parties just to tease.
In this wild garden, what fun awaits,
As laughter blooms with the sun on the slates.

Notes in a Silent Air

Birds compose tunes filled with silly grace,
While a cat croons softly, it's quite a face.
Mice in tuxedos dance on the floor,
While the flowers gossip, wishing for more.

A breeze whistles tunes that tickle the ear,
Cupcakes on clouds, who would dare to steer?
In the hush, there's a chuckle, a sweet little sigh,
Even the sky can't help but comply.

The Stillness Between Thoughts

In a world where thoughts collide,
Socks and sandals take a ride.
Birds chirp jokes among the trees,
While ants debate on flying fees.

Clouds fluff pillows in the sky,
As squirrels ponder, 'Why oh why?'
Lazily, the sun yawns wide,
And laziness becomes our guide.

Rabbits hop while turtles scheme,
In the land where we all dream.
Why rush when cows are so serene?
They're experts in the art of... cuisine?

So settle down, enjoy the tease,
Life's too short, let's just freeze.
A moment's pause, a laugh, a sigh,
In this stillness, let's just lie.

When Time Ceases to Rush

Tick-tock goes the lazy clock,
Jellybeans play hopscotch on the dock.
Time decided it would take a break,
And now the mice are baking cake.

Daisies are teaching drills to bees,
While the sun begs for some more Z's.
Days wander like a funny cat,
While clock hands dance in a silly spat.

Fish wear hats, and birds wear shoes,
The world is full of playful snooze.
When seconds stretch like taffy sweet,
Socks become the best of treats.

So let us linger, give a cheer,
For time that doddles, never fear.
In this space, we'll laugh till dusk,
And crown ourselves as royalty—just!

Sons and Daughters of Calm

In a land where giggles might just reign,
Turtles breakdance in the pouring rain.
The moon tells stories to the breeze,
While grass tickles bees, oh what a tease!

Kites are snaring whispers in the sky,
As vegetables plot their next banana pie.
Waves chuckle as they kiss the shore,
While seagulls argue, 'Why not more?'

Pillows float on clouds so bright,
As children chase the day and night.
We're the steady, quirky crew,
Finding joys in squishy shoes.

So join us, friends, in sweet delight,
As laughter bubbles up so bright.
In the realm where calm is key,
We'll feast on joy unceasingly!

Nature's Gentle Embrace

In the garden of absurd, we play,
Where carrots greet you and wish you day.
Butterflies sport a tango dance,
While flowers giggle in a trance.

Trees wear hats made of silly leaves,
As rabbits gather for the heaves.
The air smells like toasted marshmallow,
And all birds sing via soft cello.

Honeybees in leather jackets buzz,
While frogs discuss the latest fuzz.
Nature's humor is surely grand,
As chuckles sprinkle through the land.

So let us dance, let's spin and twirl,
In this embrace, let laughter swirl.
With nature's charm and wit so bright,
We'll paint our world in pure delight.

Moonlit Serenity

The moon gave a wink, oh what a sight,
Bats in capes, ready for flight.
Turtles in shades, they strut with flair,
Whispering secrets without a care.

Cows dance under disco lights,
Mice in tuxedos, such silly sights.
Songs of crickets, a bug's serenade,
In this calm, the odd parade.

Starlit Whispers

Under stars that gleam and shine,
A cat plays chess with a cackling swine.
A grasshopper sings, it's quite the joke,
While rabbits join in, they all bespoke.

Fireflies flicker, like tiny hopes,
Frogs in a band, they play and lope.
The night air chuckles, with every sound,
In this goofy realm, peace is found.

The Art of Unspoken Grace

A turtle in slippers takes a stroll,
While wise old owls keep control.
Squirrels flip, practicing ballet,
As the breeze carries laughter their way.

Grass blades sway, like the finest dance,
A snail in a bowtie takes a chance.
Whispers of joy beneath the trees,
Where nature giggles with utmost ease.

Reverence Among the Willows

Willows sway with tipsy cheer,
As hedgehogs toast with a can of beer.
Pigs in pajamas, what a sight,
While geese keep marching, holding tight.

Stars applaud the antics below,
A goat does yoga, quite the show.
In this odd kingdom, delight's awake,
Where even the worms join in the shake.

Omens of the Unseen

In the garden, gnomes conspire,
Whispering secrets, fueled by desire.
A hedgehog holds court, a judge so dear,
As daisies debate what's wrong and right here.

The frogs take a vote, casting shadows with pride,
While ants in their suits hustle home to hide.
A snail runs for mayor, but nobody cares,
For the path's full of wiggles and midair flares.

Escape to the Unspoken

The skies turn purple, a mystical hue,
The trees gossip softly, just for a few.
A parrot, so sassy, spills all the tea,
On the plots of the squirrels that never can flee.

Clouds float like pillows, so whimsically light,
While rabbits debate if they'll hop left or right.
With carrots as currency, they barter and trade,
While the ghosts of past bunnies serenely wade.

Shelter of Sighs

Beneath the great oak, the wise owl observes,
As bumblebees hum in their endless curves.
A turtle's slow lecture leaves all in a daze,
As the wind takes a selfie in sunbeams' gaze.

In shadows, the daisies throw wild little shindigs,
While woodland squirrels spin tales like old kings.
The chipmunks bring snacks made of nuts and of glee,
For the merry old critters who just want to be free.

The Subtle Breath of Morning

With dawn breaks a canvas, colors collide,
A rooster in pajamas makes dreams his guide.
The sun yawns awake, scratching drowsy eyes,
As butterflies giggle, dancing in the skies.

In mugs made of acorns, hot cocoa is served,
To rabbits in bow ties, who feel so unnerved.
The mornings are silly, with giggles and cheer,
And the mystery of toast that always disappears.

Luminous Quietude

In a land where socks don't hide,
The trees wear hats, quite dignified.
Birds in coats of polka dots,
Debate about the best teapots.

Butterflies dance with a flair,
Baking cakes with imaginary air.
Squirrels argue over acorn loot,
While turtles play their tiny flute.

Underneath the Starry Veil

Stars shaped like jellybeans glow bright,
As aliens showcase their dance tonight.
Worms in tuxedos do the twist,
While frogs climb trees, as if they missed.

The moon is made of cheesy bread,
A tasty treat for dreams half-spread.
Crickets chirp in perfect rhyme,
Talking nonsense about the time.

Enchanted Stillness

In gardens where the teapots sing,
Lemons play chess with a butterfly king.
Rabbits juggle carrots with zest,
While the frost fairies take a rest.

The goldfish swim in lakes of glue,
Rehearsing lines for their debut.
Wandering clouds wear silly hats,
Tickling the noses of sleepy cats.

The Dawn of Gentle Whispers

At dawn, the socks begin to cheer,
As cats in gowns appear so sheer.
Clouds roll in like candyfloss,
While roosters play the game of toss.

Pancakes flip, and syrup sings,
The sun arrives with sparkly rings.
Meadowlarks put on a show,
As daisies stomp, putting on a glow.

Echoes of Tranquility

In a land where llamas dance,
And trees all wear a silly hat,
The crickets sing in funny prance,
While squirrels engage in chitchat.

Butterflies with tuba skills,
Play tunes that tickle on the breeze,
While daisies share their leafy thrills,
With giggles hiding in the leaves.

The sun winks from a cloud of fluff,
And whispers secrets to the bugs,
As monkeys redefine the tough,
In games of rolling in the rugs.

So if you seek a place of glee,
Where laughter echoes through the trees,
Join in the joyful jubilee,
In a paradise of happy bees.

A Haven for the Heart

In a spot where turtles read,
And daisies brew their herbal tea,
Bees wear shades and take the lead,
In dance parties under the tree.

Cats with hats solve puzzles, too,
While frogs engage in limbo gold,
And flowers play a game or two,
In tales that never grow too old.

The sky's a canvas, colors bright,
As paint-splattered clouds drift along,
While all creatures, day or night,
Join in a chorus, sweet and strong.

So bring your woes and leave them there,
At this haven of delight,
Where love and laughter fill the air,
And every heart can take to flight.

Murmurs Beneath the Canopy

Underneath the leafy dome,
Where giggles weave through whispers low,
A cheeky squirrel steals a comb,
And pranks the birds who start to crow.

The owls play chess with eager mice,
While fireflies play hide and seek,
In nature's gym of softest spice,
They sprout a hint of playful cheek.

The brook narrates a goofy tale,
Of fish who wear the finest bling,
While turtles race, but just for sale,
In lavish dreams of summer fling.

So come and listen, feel the cheer,
In whispers soft and winks from trees,
This place where humor's crystal clear,
Invites the funny heart with ease.

Traces of Celestial Calm

In a cosmos where cats can fly,
And moonbeams wear a mist of glee,
Each star has jokes that touch the sky,
And comets roll in cupcake spree.

The sun plays hopscotch with a wink,
While planets giggle in their orbits,
As stardust throws a quirky pink,
In confetti trails — no one forbids.

Galaxies spin like cunning yo-yos,
And meteors dance on cosmic ground,
While nebulae wear floral bows,
In this place where joy is found.

So lift your spirits, gaze above,
Where laughter twinkles bright and clear,
In this realm of smiles and love,
You'll find the calm that's filled with cheer.

A Haven of Soft Sunlight

In the garden, gnomes play tag,
Chasing shadows, oh, such a rag!
Bunnies beam with little pride,
As flowers dance, their stems they glide.

Sunbeams tickle each leaf's face,
While ants march in a silly race.
Who knew the daisies could do splits?
Just wait till twilight—oh, the bits!

Step aside, the cat's in charge,
Planning mischief, oh so large.
Birds gossip on the old tree's limb,
Echoing laughter on a whim.

With laughter loud, the breeze takes flight,
As squirrels throw acorns—what a sight!
In this haven of warm delight,
Even the moon can't help but smile bright.

The Quietude of Distant Shores

Seashells whisper in the sand,
Seagulls steal fries, oh, how they band!
Crabs have got their dance moves down,
And seaweed teases fish to frown.

Palm trees sway with a cheeky grin,
While sunburnt tourists give a spin.
The beach ball bounces, oh so high,
But lands on someone's sandwich—my, oh my!

Sandcastles here resemble blobs,
As children battle with their mobs.
But watch out for that sneaky wave,
It'll take your bucket like a knave!

With laughter ringing in the air,
The sun just grins, it doesn't care.
In this realm of silly shores,
Life's a joke, and joy restores!

Dusk's Tender Grasp

As day turns orange, birds take flight,
Chasing shadows that look just right.
Fireflies blink in a friendly prank,
While crickets chirp—life's on the flank.

The sun bows down with a wink,
While raccoons plot, just let them think.
Twilight tickles tall lampposts bright,
As stars pop out, gleeful at night.

A chatty owl gives wise advice,
While hedgehogs roll—oh, isn't it nice?
In dusk's embrace, the world's at play,
As laughter dances, fading away.

The horizon's open for silly dreams,
Where nothing's ever quite as it seems.
In this tender twilight, rest your head,
Tomorrow brings more mischief instead!

Harmony in the Void

In the stillness, cats make noise,
Purring symphonies, oh, what joys!
Between the cushions, secrets lie,
As shoes embark on a sly goodbye.

Lost socks giggle in hidden lanes,
While the fridge hums its refrains.
Cushions bounce when nobody's near,
A ghostly ballet, oh dear, oh dear!

The ceiling fan spins tales, they say,
Of dust bunnies that dance, come what may.
Harmony stirs in playful rounds,
Each little whimsy in silence sounds.

So tiptoe gently through the night,
Where pillows hold a thousand delights.
In this quiet, what can you find?
A world where laughter's unconfined!

A Tapestry of Calm Moments

In the green patch, a gnome did yawn,
He twisted his beard at the break of dawn.
A squirrel wore socks, quite a funky sight,
And teased the birds at the morning light.

The turtles played cards, their shells in bloom,
While frogs cracked jokes, dispelling the gloom.
A picnic was held by the bubbling brook,
Where ants served cake from their little cookbook.

Breezes whispered secrets to each passing leaf,
While bees hummed tunes of a comic relief.
A sunflower chuckled, tipping its head,
As the daisies danced, their laughter widespread.

So in these moments, with giggles and glee,
Nature's a jester, not just you and me.
Laughter erupts in this whimsical place,
Where joy takes its seat and wears a big face.

Nature's Serenade in Stillness

A snail in a top hat slid down the trail,
With a wink and a grin, he told a tall tale.
The butterflies giggled, all dressed up in dots,
Avoiding the mud, and the splashes of blots.

An owl wore glasses, perched high on a branch,
Reading a book and plotting his ranch.
While the grasshoppers jazzed with sweet little beats,
And the groundhogs formed a line—what a treat!

The daisies held hands, and the daisies did sway,
To the rhythm of nature, in their own way.
Then a raccoon slid by, with a pie on its back,
Claiming it was his—it was quite the whack!

So here in this place, with antics galore,
Nature sings praises we couldn't ignore.
With chuckles and giggles, and joyful outcries,
Every living creature wears laughter as ties.

Unveiling the Silent Wonders

In a nook of the woods, a bear lost its way,
Consulted a map, and said, "Let's play!"
While rabbits debated on the best veggie stew,
The hedgehogs planned a hide-and-seek too.

A fish in a pond, wearing a crown of moss,
Declared himself king with a dizzying gloss.
The frogs did the cha-cha, their legs in a twist,
As the fireflies glimmered, they could not resist.

A raccoon with flair served snacks on a plate,
While monkeys swung by, shouting, "Isn't this great?"
They juggled ripe apples, their laughter went far,
In this world of whimsy, they raised the bizarre.

So in this stillness, with cheer in the air,
Nature unfolds wonders beyond compare.
With giggles and snickers that fill every nook,
The secrets of joys are found in each nook.

Where Shadows Dance in Peace

Under the tree where shadows play tricks,
A raccoon played chess—it's quite a fix!
The owls made rules, declaring a draw,
While the rabbits laughed, "Hey, we saw that flaw!"

An ant in a hat gave a motivational speech,
Proclaiming that dreams are within our reach.
The crickets chirped tunes of great jubilation,
As the moon joined in for the night's celebration.

The shadows exchanged glances; they named a new dance,
Practicing twirls, giving it a chance.
With a jig and a wiggle, they swayed to and fro,
In a world where silliness is sure to glow.

So here in this space, where laughter does soar,
Each creature joins in, they can't help but explore.
In this dance of delight, with shadows as friends,
The humor of nature, it never quite ends.

The Beauty of Absence

In a garden with no weeds,
The gnomes dance with such speed.
No noise to break the charm,
Just frogs with a croak that's calm.

The birds forgot to sing here,
They sit tight without fear.
Even the sun wears shades,
Not a peep in the sun's glades.

The flowers hold a meeting,
On petals, secrets fleeting.
Their giggles softly swirl,
As daisies do a twirl.

Absence makes the heart grow fonder,
Each silence is a wonder.
With not a sound in sight,
Commotion takes a flight!

Silent Resplendence

In fields where silence thrives,
The crickets play with their drives.
No chatter on the breeze,
Just whispered giggles from trees.

The clouds wear silly hats,
And gather like friendly chats.
They float by with a grin,
While the sun gives a cheeky spin.

The petals play peek-a-boo,
With colors bright and true.
In stillness, jokes unfold,
As flowers trade tales bold.

What joy in this hush so light,
Where stars giggle, oh what a sight!
Every breeze brings a slapstick,
In the calm, it's pure comic trick!

Petals of Peace

Petals on the water glide,
As fish pretend to hide.
But their laughter's clear as day,
In this pond where frogs play.

The sun throws sparkles at the shore,
With giggles that ask for more.
A squirrel steals a nut with flair,
While flowers gasp in fresh air.

The bees wear tiny suits to dance,
Over blossoms, they prance.
In absence, chaos takes a break,
As leaves joke and silently shake.

Finding glee in every space,
Where calmness finds its place.
The joy is soft, not loud,
In petals, the stillness is proud!

Finding Home in Still Waters

Ripples skip like cheerful dreams,
While the fish laugh in teams.
Turtles sunbathe with a wink,
In stillness, there's much to think.

The lilies gossip, heads held high,
Wondering who'll pass by.
The dragonflies wear coats of sheen,
In still waters, they reign supreme.

Each splash is a comic show,
As nature puts on quite the flow.
With every glance, a punchline found,
In this silence, joy abounds.

Home is where the giggles rise,
In stillness, laughter flies.
So here we laugh and play our part,
In a world full of silent art!

Celestial Calm

In a realm where clouds play hide and seek,
The sun wears shades, feeling quite weak.
Birds gossip softly, sharing a grin,
While turtles compete, who's last to begin.

Laughter flows like streams in the air,
Butterflies gossip without a care.
Breezes tickle flowers, they dance and twirl,
As squirrels chuckle, giving life a whirl.

A starlit picnic with sandwiches square,
Aliens drop by, claiming they're rare.
With wobbly chairs, they sit in a row,
As wise frogs croak jokes that steal the show.

Life's hilarious here, with nothing amiss,
Even the moon gives a comical kiss.
So here we dwell, in whimsy's embrace,
In a paradise bright, laughter fills the space.

A Symphony of Sighs

The trees serenade with an off-key song,
The rhythm of crickets never feels wrong.
A breeze plays drums on the rustling leaves,
As frogs join in, practicing for thieves.

Turtles trudge along, slow as they please,
While rabbits debate, 'To jump or to freeze?'
The stars snicker down, wearing jester hats,
Inviting the owls to throw down their stats.

The moon rolls its eyes at the comic scene,
As fireflies flicker, like lights on a screen.
A laughter-filled night, wrapped in soft charms,
Where every sigh feels like hugs in warm arms.

With popcorn in hand, the night takes its flight,
As shadows dance joyfully, bathed in moonlight.
A symphony played where giggles collide,
In the heart of this jest, joy cannot hide.

Reverie in the Meadow

A meadow of whimsy where daisies wink,
Buttercups tease, and nobody thinks.
The clouds wear frowns, just a bit out of shape,
As bees laugh while fashioning honey drape.

A snail joins a race, feeling quite spry,
With grass blades as hurdles, he aims for the sky.
The daisies giggle, their petals in bloom,
While hidden gophers plan a sweetly mad loom.

A pensive cow ponders the meaning of haste,
As chickens play poker, time there's no waste.
The wind brings tickles from far-off away,
While frogs discuss philosophy, day after day.

An orchestra of nonsense plays life's song,
As butterflies hop and butterflies throng.
In this reverie, humor's the heart,
In a meadow where silly is simply an art.

Shadows of Peaceful Retreats

In corners of calm where the laughter is deep,
The shadows blend in, doing funny leaps.
Giant mushrooms giggle, their tops all askew,
As raccoons plan parties, oh what a view!

A sunbeam drapes over a sleepy old bear,
While otters float by, not a single care.
Tadpoles throw parties, their dance off the charts,
As wise old owls offer questionable arts.

The leaves play chess, pretending to think,
With squirrels as referees, shouting "Don't blink!"
Even the breeze wears a comically grin,
Infusing the woodlands with chuckles within.

In these retreats where the shadows are light,
Everyone's welcome to stay for the night.
With jokes whispering softly through branches and brush,
The humor of nature, forever in hush.

Hushed Harmonies

In the garden, gnomes do dance,
With moves that leave us in a trance.
They twirl and tumble, a sight so rare,
While squirrels judge from their leafy chair.

A snail tries hard to make a dash,
But in slow motion, it's quite the clash.
The bunnies giggle, tails in the air,
As plants gossip, 'Oh, what a pair!'

Embrace of Gentle Breezes

The wind whispers jokes to flowers bright,
They chuckle softly, what a delight!
In the shade of trees, a worm took a nap,
Dreaming of cheese in a big old trap.

Butterflies laugh, flapping their wings,
As ladybugs join in on silly things.
A bright red beetle tries to sing,
But falls off the leaf, oh, the chaos it brings!

Solitude's Embrace

A toad on a rock sings very off-key,
In harmony with a buzzing bumblebee.
With crickets as backup, they put on a show,
While frogs roll their eyes, 'Oh no, here we go!'

The sun yawns wide, stretching its rays,
As ants march by in a comical craze.
One drops a crumb, oh what a scene,
A feast for a mouse, the tiniest cuisine!

Reflections in Still Waters

The pond reflects a cat's silly face,
Who thinks it's a fierce, majestic ace.
But a splash from the fish shows them who's boss,
As it bubbles up while the cat plays toss.

Frogs sit in circles, laughing at fate,
Joking about flies they eagerly sate.
A duck quacks loudly, "I'm the star here!"
While the fish reply, "You're just full of cheer!"

Garden of Whispered Hope

In a garden where whispers bloom,
Plants gossip under the moon.
The daisies chuckle, the roses tease,
While the sunflowers dance in a gentle breeze.

The carrots wear hats, all quite absurd,
Listening to the babbling bird.
Bees with monocles sip their tea,
Laughing at the trees, oh what glee!

Frogs in bow ties play chess by the brook,
While mushrooms read tales from a storybook.
And here's a fish sporting a crown,
Holding court with a grin, never a frown!

This garden is where silliness reigns,
Where laughter and joy pump through the veins.
So come take a stroll, join the fun,
Bring your own laughs, there's room for everyone!

The Breath of Celestial Fields

In fields where giggles sprout from the ground,
Cotton candy clouds dance all around.
A cow in pajamas croaks out a tune,
While butterflies throw a bright balloon soon.

The corn cobs gossip and trade tall tales,
Of romance between daisies and whistling snails.
With hiccups and chuckles, the crickets perform,
While shadows of clouds create a soft storm.

The sun wears shades on its radiant face,
Spreading cheer with flair and grace.
In this silly realm, nothing's askew,
Where laughter is golden and skies are blue!

So come to these fields with laughter and cheer,
You might catch a smile or lend them an ear.
Embrace the absurd, let your wild spirit glide,
In the breath of these fields, let joy be your guide!

Lullabies of a Dreaming World

In a world where dreams wear polka-dot shoes,
And sleepy clouds share whimsical news.
Pillows are laughing, they bounce on a bed,
While kittens and puppies play tag on your head.

The moon hums softly, a playful refrain,
As stars toss confetti like it's a game.
Teddy bears slumber with hats and good books,
Spreading sweet dreams with adorable looks.

A gentle breeze tickles the blankets so tight,
Making shadows dance, oh what a sight!
While frogs in pajamas recite silly rhymes,
Counting their laughs to pass the sweet times.

In this dreamy world, wonders unfold,
With giggles and whispers worth more than gold.
So tuck in your dreams, let the silliness stay,
In lullabies that'll brighten your day!

Starlit Tranquility

Under a sky where the stars play chess,
With planets that wear their Sunday best.
A silly comet zips past with a grin,
Shooting star wishes, let the fun begin!

The owls wear glasses, reading the night,
Telling tall tales in the soft, pale light.
While fireflies giggle, glowing with glee,
Winking at lovers by the old oak tree.

The night is a canvas of laughter and dreams,
With twinkling lights crafting whimsical themes.
Galaxies swirl in this goofy ballet,
As the universe chuckles and sings all the way!

So bask in the glow of this starlit play,
Where silliness dances and worries drift away.
In this charming expanse, love's free to bloom,
As the cosmos shares joy that brightens the gloom!

Surrendering to the Breeze

A gentle gust takes off my hat,
I chase it down, imagine that!
It tickles my ear with a playful tease,
This cheeky wind, it does as it please.

The trees are giggling, leaves a-shake,
A dandelion dance, what a mistake!
I try to sip from my iced tea,
But a rogue fly makes a meal of me.

Sunshine warms my goofy grin,
Nature's joke makes me spin!
Clouds above share winks and sighs,
While rabbits frolic in disguise.

I surrender to the breezy fun,
As laughter merges with the sun.
So join the play, oh friends, oh pals,
In this sunny world where joy just prowls.

Soft Footfalls on a Quiet Path

I tiptoe on this secret trail,
Avoiding rocks that make me wail.
A squirrel mocks my shuffling beat,
As I trip over my own two feet.

The daisies peek up with friendly grins,
Awaiting tales of my clumsy spins.
With twigs and leaves stuck in my shoe,
I'm quite the sight for this view, it's true.

A robin chuckles at my plight,
"Watch your step!" it chirps with light.
But every fall and every slip,
Is just a part of this laughing trip.

So off I go, a wobbly dream,
With soft footfalls, or so it seems.
Nature's path, a stage for glee,
In this silly, graceful jamboree!

The Beauty in Hush

In stillness, raccoons tiptoe around,
As I stumble into a soft mound.
They blink in shock, then bounce away,
Echoing laughter in the crisp day.

Birds whisper sweet gossip to each other,
While flowers giggle, 'Is that his mother?'
The silence breaks in humorous hues,
Nature's quips fill the morning views.

I pause to breathe in the leafy green,
Oh! Did that banana just scream?
I shrug it off, a new paradigm,
As ants parade, their own prime-time.

This hush is laced with vibrant jest,
Nature's laughter, oh how it's blessed!
So embrace the calm, laugh a little,
In the stillness, life's a playful riddle.

Windows to the Soul's Rest

A sleepy owl peers from its nook,
With judging eyes, it gives me a look.
"Are you lost, or just unwise?"
I shrug and smile, to my own surprise.

The stars above wink in delight,
With moonbeams painting the night bright.
What secrets they carry, I'm eager to know,
But first, I'll sweep away this crow.

It caws and flutters with quite the show,
"How dare you interfere with my glow?"
A battle of antics under the sky,
While frogs chime in, oh my! Oh my!

These windows are filled with nightly cheer,
Nature's comedy, loud and clear.
So come on in, make yourself at home,
In this goofy nook, we'll laugh and roam.

Traces of Timelessness

In a land where socks find their pairs,
And pigeons dance without any cares,
The sun wears a hat, the moon wears a grin,
As we sip lemonade with a cheeky spin.

Cats in sunglasses lounge on the grass,
Chasing their tails as the moments pass,
Clock hands are giggling, spinning around,
In this playful realm where joy is unbound.

Trees tell tall tales of the clouds above,
While bumblebees buzz in a chorus of love,
Worms do their yoga, stretching all night,
In a timeless space that's just pure delight.

We laugh with the daisies, share silly dreams,
Where nothing is serious, or so it seems,
In this dreamy world where nonsense prevails,
The traces of laughter fill up all the trails.

Calm Amongst the Chaos

Amid the rush of a busy street,
A sloth in shades finds its cozy seat,
It orders coffee, takes a nice sip,
While the world around it does a quick flip.

Llamas in suits hold a boardroom chat,
Debating the merits of wearing a hat,
While squirrels throw acorns like it's a game,
Creating a ruckus but never a shame.

In this whirly world where giggles stay,
The balloons find reasons to float away,
Kites tangle with dreams in the light of day,
And silk ribbons dance like they're here to play.

Amidst all the madness, laughter will bloom,
As we spin in circles, making our room,
The calm of the ludicrous wraps 'round our minds,
In this whimsical chaos, delight surely finds.

Lullabies of the Universe

Stars in pajamas hum a sweet tune,
While meteors play tag with the lazy moon,
A comet winks and says, 'Look at me!'
While galaxies sip on their cosmic tea.

Planets are jiving, swirling in space,
With rockets doing the cha-cha with grace,
In this nightly dance, all worries dissolve,
As we giggle at quirks that the heavens solve.

The dark whispers secrets that tickle the night,
While comets tell stories of incredible flight,
Jupiter's giggling, Saturn's wearing a crown,
In this universe, there's no way to frown.

With lullabies sung by the stars all aglow,
The universe chuckles with each little show,
In this vastness of wonder, it's clear and profound,
Laughter and dreams are where joy will abound.

Solace Found in Shadows

Beneath the tree where the shadows convene,
A wise old turtle tells jokes like a queen,
The grass shakes its head, laughing so hard,
While ants carry crumbs like a food boulevard.

In the shade, the critters all gather around,
A gopher's got gossip that's simply profound,
The wind joins the banter, spinning tales bright,
Of squirrels who thought they could dance through the night.

Bats play charades, flapping with flair,
Creating a ruckus, without any care,
While fireflies twinkle, lighting up the game,
In this sanctuary where laughter's the aim.

In the corners of dusk, where shadows reside,
The fun never ends, and the giggles abide,
Solace in silliness, we all convene,
In the heart of the whispers, we reign as the scene.

A Symphony of Restful Hues

In a land where the cows wear shades,
And the garden gnomes play charades.
Chirping crickets compose a tune,
While the sun nods off behind the moon.

Birds in bow ties take their flight,
Spreading laughter, day and night.
Squirrels juggling acorns with flair,
Make the trees chuckle, so rare!

Mice in picnics with bread and cheese,
Enjoy the breeze like they own the keys.
As daisies dance in silly tune,
Should we join them? Oh, what a boon!

Nature's jesters, what a troupe,
In this land of giggles and hoopla, we stoop.
Catch the whimsy, the joy, the sighs,
Under the winks of the fluffy skies.

Dwelling in Unseen Bliss

There's a rabbit who tells tales with flair,
Wearing a tutu and pink bunny hair.
Every evening he grins with glee,
As the ants host a tea party, you see!

Butterflies in tutus twirl about,
With wind as their partner, they dance and shout.
A frog croaks jokes, he's the king of puns,
Ribbiting laughter under golden suns.

Clouds take turns to impersonate,
Fluffy sheep, oh, what a fate!
Chasing rainbows with a goofy stride,
In a realm where chuckles collide.

So sip your tea from a mushroom cup,
While we watch the wild hiccup up.
Here, the silly never ceases,
In this place where giggles increase!

Reflections on Stillness

In a pond where fish wear monocles grand,
And turtles play chess on the warm sand.
The frogs leap in laughter, oh so spry,
While dragonflies zip, "Did you see me fly?"

The reeds whisper secrets, quite absurd,
While the chicken lays eggs that prefer to be bird.
Each moment is full of gentle jest,
Even the crickets in bowties look their best.

A snail takes a selfie, striking a pose,
While the bear munches berries, nose in those.
Laughs and snorts echo, the frogs agree,
This stillness is full of whimsical glee!

So here we gather, under a tree,
Where silliness blooms like a pot of honey.
Join the frolic, take off your frown,
In this calm, wear your joy like a crown!

Secrets of a Serene Realm

Worms in jackets hold court in the dirt,
While snails throw parties, dressed in dessert.
Here giggles sprout like daisies in spring,
Even the toads know how to sing!

Ladybugs in ballet shoes prance,
Spinning and twirling, come join the dance!
The sun chuckles softly, lighting the scene,
While trees crack jokes about being so green.

A wise old owl with spectacles perched,
Teaching squirrels, as giggles are church'd.
In this land, even the flowers grin,
As laughter unfurls from within to spin.

So take a moment, breathe in the lore,
Where mirth is the key, opening a door.
With every tickle of breeze that we find,
We'll share this joy, leaving worries behind!

Hallowed Ground of Rest

In a field where grass won't sneeze,
Ants are dancing with the bees.
Clouds wear hats, so very silly,
As they float by, looking frilly.

A cat in shades takes a long nap,
While a dog attempts a yoga lap.
Squirrels giggle as they tease,
Swapping nuts with cat-like ease.

Bunnies hop in two-step pairs,
Sharing tales of their wild hair flares.
The sun winks from its golden throne,
As laughter snickers, all alone.

Here joy blooms without a care,
In a jolly, whimsical affair.
With each tickle of the breeze,
Life's a picnic, if you please!

Breath of the Untouched

Whispers ride on fluttering wings,
Where the moon giggles, and softly sings.
Frogs in tuxedos croak with flair,
Toads twirl round like they just don't care.

The stars play hopscotch, their lights aglow,
While fireflies imitate a show.
Jellybeans rain from candy trees,
Such magic, it brings you to your knees!

Breezes tickle the dandelion heads,
Planting wishes in colorful beds.
A parrot plays chess with the breeze,
And the grass claps along with ease.

Every shadow's an impromptu dance,
In this world of whimsical chance.
Where goofiness whirls with delight,
And makes every heart feel light!

In the Arms of Nature's Peace

On a pillow of moss, all snug and tight,
Crickets hold karaoke all night.
Mice in tuxes prepare for a show,
As the snails set the scene, row by row.

Ducks wear bow ties, strutting about,
While the otters gossip, swimming in doubt.
The trees chuckle at a squirrel's tease,
As the wind whispers jokes through the leaves.

Pillows of clouds hold a pillow fight,
With feathers drifting as stars take flight.
Nature's theater, a comical spree,
Where every critter plays for free!

Here, laughs echo in every nook,
As a porcupine writes a funny book.
In the arms of this jolly embrace,
Silly smiles steer the tranquil space!

Murmurs of the Heart

On a swing made of twigs sways a crow,
Rapping the rhythm with a soft row.
The lilies giggle, swaying in time,
As frogs recite their favorite rhyme.

A turtle dashes at a snail's pace,
In this world without a race.
The sun-chased shadows do a conga line,
Creating chuckles under the pine.

Laughter bubbles from a bubbling brook,
As turtles ponder the next big hook.
Whiskers twitch from a cheeky cat,
The joy of this place is where it's at!

With every murmur, a chuckle flies,
Where the whimsical nature never lies.
It fills the air with giggles, so sweet,
In this blessed land, where joy's complete!

Shadows in the Twilight

When dusk creeps in, the shadows play,
They trip on toes, then run away.
Laughter floats through evening air,
Even squirrels stop and stare.

The moon wears glasses, quite a sight,
As stars engage in a pillow fight.
The crickets sing the loudest tune,
While owls hoot, 'Is that a balloon?'

A cat in a bus, quite a feat,
Chasing a dog on tiny feet.
They laugh, they chase, all through the grass,
And time just slips right through their class.

In shadows deep, the laughter grows,
A secret dance that nobody knows.
And in the twilight, jokes unfold,
As silly tales of wonder told.

The Respite in Bloom

A flower sneezes—achoo! It sings,
A bumblebee dons tiny wings.
They chatter 'bout the hot spring sun,
And practice having lots of fun.

The daisies wear their polka dots,
As giggles float from merry pots.
The tulips giggle, quite absurd,
While roses blush, then share a word.

Butterflies wear hats askew,
A fashion show? Oh yes, who knew!
They twirl and spin, a colorful sight,
While sunbeams compete in sheer delight.

In this garden, joy's the theme,
With petals dancing in a dream.
Every bloom, a silly quest,
In nature's laugh, we feel the best.

Gentle Accompaniment

A mouse plays tunes on cheese-filled pipes,
While ants march by in goofy stripes.
A melody of giggles springs,
As frogs join in and croak like kings.

A cloud drifts by with cotton candy,
And shepherds lead with banjo handy.
The wind joins in, a whistling sound,
As all of nature spins around.

The crickets hum in harmony,
While daisies dance to revelry.
Each note a giggle, each beat a cheer,
In this grand band, there's nothing to fear!

Here every leaf is a maraca,
And every bloom a lively araka.
Together, they play, the show must start,
With laughter woven into the heart.

Emptiness Dances with Light

In a hall of echoes, light tiptoes,
Whispering jokes that nobody knows.
A shadow trips, then starts to grin,
And playfully pulls the sun right in.

The scenery giggles, old doors will creak,
As silence hums with a squeaky squeak.
The walls are papered with smiles and glee,
While emptiness sways like a shrubbery.

Dim corners join in the swirly show,
With flickering lights putting on a glow.
The floor's made of laughter, each step a cue,
And twinkling stars join just for you!

In spaces vast, where silliness reigns,
A cosmic dance in grand refrains.
Emptiness bows, and light takes the lead,
In this whimsical waltz, we all succeed!

Whispers of Eden

In a garden where veggies tease,
Tomatoes joke with bumblebees,
Lettuce giggles in the breeze,
While carrots play hide and seek with trees.

The apples sit with a knowing glance,
Pears do a waltz, they love to prance,
While strawberries throw a dance-off chance,
As cucumbers plot their veggie romance.

Night comes quietly, stars make a scene,
The radishes dream of being serene,
As moonbeams giggle, and shadows glean,
Life's a laugh in this leafy marine.

With every bloom and funny sight,
Nature's humor brings pure delight,
In Eden's embrace, all feels just right,
A comedy sketch in soft moonlight.

Serenity's Embrace

In a world where daisies bake,
Silly squirrels dance and shake,
Butterflies wear hats for fun's sake,
This is no ordinary lake!

Geese debate who's the best swimmer,
While frogs add a chorus, a lively glimmer,
The sun dips low, the sky turns dimmer,
But giggles echo, no chance of a bummer.

Clouds exchange secrets, soft and light,
A cabbage patch holds a tea party tonight,
Carrots dressed up in faux fur delight,
In this cozy nook, laughter takes flight.

As twilight drapes its velvet shawl,
Whimsical dreams begin to enthrall,
With each blush and giggle, we rise and fall,
In serenity, we find joy for all.

Still Waters

A pond reflects the jokes we tell,
As fishes giggle, wishing well,
Alligators wear hats, run like hell,
Their belly flops create quite the swell!

The frogs rock out in harmony,
While turtles twirl quite comically,
A water lily's a stage, you see,
In the splash of fun, we all agree!

Crickets chirp in rhythmic beats,
The moon suggests orchestral treats,
As dragonflies bob on their tiny seats,
Nature's concert, no one retreats.

So come join in the world so bright,
Where laughter lingers in the night,
In still waters, joy takes flight,
Nature's comedy brings pure delight.

Hidden Dreams

In the woods where whispers sing,
Mice throw parties with cheese and bling,
Trees wear scarves, oh what a thing,
While shadows dance and insects cling.

The owls play chess by the moon's glow,
Squirrels debate who runs the show,
A snail wins the race, nice and slow,
In hidden dreams, joy begins to flow.

Flowers gossip about the breeze,
Sharing secrets with friendly bees,
While hidden gnomes roll on their knees,
Life's a giggle beneath the trees.

As daylight fades to a sleepy beam,
The forest chuckles, it's a grand theme,
In a haven where laughter gleams,
Hidden dreams fulfill the sweetest dreams.

The Softness of Sacred Spaces

In pillow clouds where all is bright,
Purrs of kittens fill the night,
Bunnies hop in a giggly flight,
This sacred space feels just so right.

Marshmallow trees are a child's dream,
Chocolate rivers flow like a theme,
Rainbows bend and sparkle, it seems,
In this realm of fluffy extremes.

The sun throws jokes with a golden ray,
While fairies dance and sing ballet,
Each sprout and leaf joins in the play,
In this sacred soft, they sway and sway.

At dusk, the stars cast a wink,
With whispers that make us all think,
In softness of spaces, we link,
Jovial hearts in twilight's drink.

The Silence of Blooming Orchards

In orchards where the fruits hang low,
The bees hold meetings, plotting their show.
A squirrel debates, should he leap or not,
While apples giggle, they say, "Look what we've got!"

The trees wear robes of pink and white,
Beneath them lies a sleepy sight.
A crow, with style, struts and prances,
While plums roll by in comical dances.

Crisp pears gossip 'bout which will fall first,
Tucking their leaves in, they quench their thirst.
The wind chuckles as it tickles the grass,
While cherries argue who's the juiciest sass.

So here in bloom, the laughter flows,
Among petals soft, where silliness grows.
The sun breaks through with a golden grin,
In this orchard realm, let giggles begin!

Glistening Pathways of Peace

A path made of puddles, they glimmer and shine,
With frogs in tuxedos, they dance in a line.
The daisies wave at a butterfly prince,
Who huffs and heaves, as if he can't win.

Snails in a hurry, they race for the light,
While ants hold a banquet, it's quite a delight.
Laughing out loud as the thunder rolls in,
A cloud joins the fun, with a wink, and a grin.

Breezes blow softly, but stirs up some leaves,
Tickling the grass, as if it believes.
A dandelion sneezes and spreads all its fluff,
And giggling kids say, "Hey, wasn't that tough?"

On these glistening pathways, behold the jest,
Nature engaging in a casual fest.
With smiles all around, the day carries on,
Where laughter reigns bright, from dusk until dawn.

Hushed Nightfall in Utopia

As night falls gently, the crickets compose,
A symphony crafted by those with long toes.
The moon winks down, and the stars play charades,
Whispers of laughter in the leafy cascades.

A fox wearing glasses reads tales of the day,
While owls debate, "Is it night or is it play?"
Bats zip and zoom, drawing silly designs,
As fireflies giggle lighting up hopeful signs.

The brook hums softly, "You'll never guess who,"
While willows are swaying in pajamas of dew.
A hedgehog rolls over, snorts and then snickers,
As moths hold a dance, their moves making flickers.

In the hush of the night, where shadows align,
Belief in the silly, a world so divine.
So here's a toast to the joy all around,
In this hushed utopia, pure laughter is found!

Tides of Gentle Reverie

Upon the shores where the soft waves crash,
Seagulls tell secrets with quite a loud splash.
Shells whisper tales of the sun and the foam,
While starfish dance, dreaming of home.

A crab in a tux takes a stroll by the tide,
With clams cracking jokes, they cannot abide.
The surf rolls in with a giggle and glee,
While dolphins jump high, just look and see!

The sun dips low, coloring all in delight,
Where jellyfish float, casting shadows so light.
A pelican juggles, the audience cheers,
While waves hold a concert, amid laughter and sneers.

These tides of reverie are silly yet true,
With each little creature just sharing their view.
In a world full of joy, under skies so wide,
Adventure blooms forth, like a playful tide.

The Language of Still Air

Whispers dance on tiptoes here,
As leaves debate the speed of cheer.
The breeze rolls by, with laughter mild,
Even the clouds seem quite beguiled.

In this hush, the bugs all hum,
Debating life, while trees just drum.
A squirrel jokes, a nut in tow,
While ants coordinate their grand show.

Silent moments, but oh so loud,
Nature's humor, in a shroud.
Birds crack wise, a feathered jest,
In this stillness, who needs rest?

Here every twist has comic flair,
A quiet mirth fills the air.
So let's embrace this giddy peace,
Where lullabies and laughter cease.

Soliloquy of the Stars

Stars whisper secrets, oh so bright,
Trading punchlines in the night.
One twinkling tells of mischief made,
While another's just trying to get laid.

Moon rolls its eyes at cosmic flops,
Making constellations from awkward hops.
The Milky Way spills a giggle or two,
As meteors dash with a cheeky view.

Galaxies toast to their own charm,
While comets race without a qualm.
So many jokes in this void vast,
Stellar stand-up, a blast from the past.

Who knew the night had such wit?
With every spark, a tale is split.
In this silence, wit is profound,
In celestial comedy, laughter abounds.

A Sanctuary in the Calm

In a nook where giggles hide,
Where frogs croak jokes and fish confide.
The pond ripples, a joke unspooled,
As dragonflies dance, happily schooled.

Round the bend, a turtle grins,
Sharing tales of his slow, sly wins.
The lilies nod, their petals flick,
While shadows of bumblebees perform a trick.

With every hush, there's jest aplenty,
As toads do cartwheels, all so spritely.
And though it seems a tranquil scene,
Nature's pranks are slyly keen.

In this space, calm takes a turn,
With whispers of fun that always burn.
A secret world, where jesters reign,
In this peace, joy leaves its stain.

Embracing the Soft Echoes

Echoes chatter in the cozy glade,
With every footfall, a joke is laid.
Rustling leaves giggle with the breeze,
A giggling chorus, nature's tease.

The shadows dance, tipping their hats,
While critters plot, where are the chats?
A fox let out a chuckle's glee,
As its friends join in – a comedy spree.

With each step now a clumsy affair,
Nature's jesters jump with flair.
In this silence, their laughter rings,
A world alive with joyful things.

So come and sit, play a tune,
Let nature's humor make you swoon.
With echoes soft, joy is bestowed,
In this calm, wild mirth bestowed.

www.ingramcontent.com/pod-product-compliance
Lightning Source LLC
Chambersburg PA
CBHW052221090526
44585CB00015BA/1361